SOME ALONE TIME

LAKEISHA NORISE

BookLeaf Publishing

India | USA | UK

SOME ALONE TIME © 2024 LAKEISHA NORISE

All rights reserved.

No part of this publication may be reproduced, stored in a retrieval system, or transmitted, in any form or by any means, electronic, mechanical, photocopying, recording or otherwise, without the prior written permission of the presenters.

LAKEISHA NORISE asserts the moral right to be identified as author of this work.

Presentation by *BookLeaf Publishing*

Web: www.bookleafpub.com

E-mail: info@bookleafpub.com

ISBN: 9789360945008

First edition 2024

TO MY BOYS

JaLon and Jeoni

No matter what, Mommy always loves you

Infatuation

It's the glimmer in the corner of my eye
...wait are you looking
no, okay I'm clear to have fun again
I'd rather say it's no judgement from you
That i'm not concerned about what you think
To prove to Me, you not that big of a deal
Its the thought that counts........right

Pause

nothing to reminisce
nothing to miss
Why do I act like this is somethin for you
something to make your brain crank out
emotions and feelings for me
i cant make you think
wanting my words to feel like Drake
or a family reunuion on Summar days
shirts like jerseys, matching front, matching
print
saving good times so public altercations dont
exist
still......
i feel you waiting on my words
not understanding, cocking yo head to the side
blank stare" ......what you mean"
words at my lips, so done expelling, speechless
which i'm never left in
like unconditional lovin'
raw dog, fake glovin'
Say you go that Brent faiyaz kinda feel
sounding toxic again but the girlies love it
it looks real so they really socking it up
still.....

waiting on phone calls so i'm accidentally
texting you because your nummber has been
deleted
draining, missing you, feeling depleted
ready, bothered, hot, waiting for you to feel
defeated
wanting to feel like Sperman again, again come
drown
it won;t be long now
say your home
something's better left unsaid and you ask "will
you be my girlfriend"
still.....

Summer Walkers Scissors

Who think he talking to
Who he think he getting through
Getting over you
Once again denying shit you do
It's okay,
i'll get over you anyway
whats a day
wasted money, wasted fun...that aint funny
I ain't the one
to be playing
sad to say I listen to everything you be saying

My calm/ Your Hype

You wanna address everything
I didn't see you as the DaBaby
Dressed as postmasters
but you was on a girl's stamps
Looking enveloped in somebody else's shit
Whatever makes you happy
What about sixty
all them choices you'll never have to be picky
all them chairs at the table, nobody knows
who's running things
running game, say Finese my middle name
Your main game
dont run to me because she running game on you
"you can be anything thing you want, even you"

Ask you on a date

Been in it for so long
can't turn away
told her to leave
all he u can do it stay
 dont know nothing else
scared to take a leap
scared to see
scared to peak
dont want her to speak
no new heights
no new friends
rather new dividends, current stated of
somebody else
turning green
its it jealous or vulnerablility
transparency, clarity
one step further
one step farther

Raindrop

joinging an ocean
wait you need to be here
providing life for another
no signs, no red flags
no warning, no caution
failing to earth like a nuclear bomb
exploding on impact
ahhhhhh finally
as the absorption process takes place
the nourishment
as 2 becomes 1
taking it all in
deep sighs of longing
bringing life to something that was once dead
on the brink of life
your prescence...who knew
until the it staarts over
life about it all
watching, waiting...until the day
the relsease once again
the fall

Falling up

how many times did it take you
didnt count.....
not surprised
jumping from candy stores speaking on yo
Chico stick and chocolate bars
mentioning nothin but the prize
focused your attention
keeping your mind
no big car talk
a little heavy on the drip
heavy on lips
givin flowers, no tulips, no lily
makin her laugh, acting silly, showin out so the
girlies getting excited
meanwhile she slighted
waiting
not even one nighted
embarrassed of her smile
nicknaming
finger pointing and blaming getting her caught
up
keep her busy with ya friends
how she found you in the first place
caught eyes and took up space
put her in 5th place

now she in a sick place
cant forget your face
now she aint even concerned

Killin' it

see it in her
the way she walk
where her confidence coming from Queen
cant help but to deem you royalty
its it Maybelline
gotta be something
something keeping you high
1st place pedestal love
damn
the way you stare
its not even staring....the way you glare
you taking me all in and I'm not even knowing
not guessing, feeling insecure and like you want
it
for me to put it down
not knowing its how beautiful you are
seeing the beauty in others where they cant, we
drown
you confidence saying take me now
such a good girl, your friends are bad
its not even your style
never had a one night fling
my vanity cant let you pass
my ego ready to make you my ting even though
i'm damn near doing the husband and wife thing

Options

erected spine
thousand thread count sheets
pillows reminiscent of moan escaping your blue
chakra
reciprocating my warmth
duvets and covers sprawled over my
God-lengthened extremities
spring and foam supporting my curves
not replacing, yet place holders
an existence longed for
unassuming of what exactly is missing from this
grainy feels of eye lids
usually providing cinema at this time of rotation
fine prints along my largest organ
thumping and pacing from a known source
complicated masters of minds say an emotion is
expelled here
not pausing for one beat
its my mind too fast for the goodyears on a
machine so strong
is there not enough petroleum fought for in wars
expecting my gel fill in to hold tight to
something
is the anticipation not boiling over
hot and bothered is just a phrase in your circles

Computer love

his picture is gorgeous
his hobbies are obvious
friends, thousands
family, included, all smiling
A poke
A smile
A wink
A DM
its going down like a BoneCrusher song
in laid back cheeksters
is it a screen or a block
its keeping him from knowing my natural state
relaxed, hair tied, chilling wit no make-up on
dropping digits
stolen instagram model pics
having church functions...yeah catfish
He still gone love this
nice booty, big tits
taken in in all the right places
he gon love the way he fits
Face is a plus
just never know what it is
never works out at parties, clubs or my friends
picnics
when he so fine he make me blush

my personality and sense of humor is so clutch
lifestyle choices okay maybe I did too much
All I know is he is not just wanting to fuck
He keep texting me
Nope I'm not ready
He just want to take me to lunch
Why he like me? He got hoes by the bunch
okay Its not that heavy
Stop trippin and being all sweaty
He wants to take you out and have fun already
Liking status and news feed riding like waves
back and forth got you giggling to yourself
all you can think about is "im not gone cave in"
Posting selfies in famlilar places
not hearing your voice yet
"wanna meet up"
just say yes
you get dressed
call your girls up cause you stay stressed
show em ya fit, all they say "yaaaaaassssss"
feelin good you step out
your empty apartment waits your return
you show up and there is talking with his friend
you came alone, a not-so easy feeling
turning around, he catches your step
" hey you"
looking down and glance up at his innocent
smile

Illinois has nothing on your conversation with
your shoes
his eyes spread wide
unbelievable thoughts flood his mind, downing
out the doubt
giving his homeboy the knod as he walks out
grinning
knowing what this is meaning
not feighning, not dreaming
laughing and cackling fills the air
.....he found you

Body Neighborhood

looking like trees
bobbing and weaving
coming and going
flowing
covering the brain
ziplining the insdides of the body
carrying everything from bloodlines to diseases
if too much, if too thick
within it, everything ceases
shockwaves from one powerline to the other
take off work, one needs to recover
helping out, love from a lover
a family member or another
a network speaking without words
everything that needs to be done is still heard

Brick House

cracked foundation
speaking and knocking on wood
opening closed doors
slamming windows
broken doorknobs still turning
gas furnace still burning
family every Sunday still returning
all the pain still blurring
funny stories of pigs and their sticks
building house providing for themselves and yet
something in the day wanting a kernel of your
cob
big cars parked in an open garage
can me it smart now and just use a fob
making a house a home

Notebook

chills up my spine
areolas erect
goosebumps on my skin
is it a touch
its a thought
a random car riding past
could it be you
you're not on my mind
emotions in check
Haven't let you in
I'm done, I've had enough
Any left of you is a lot
I got over you way too fast
Just something I do

Bushy-haired love

18

Glistening eyes
catching my mind
actions like sweet poetry
waves in grass
riding on surfboards of your body
cloud watching
sunbeam gazing
warming my existence
a sense of scent
lingering
nothing pin-pointing how
strawberry cream chocolate
not need the whole box
chose like a premonition
pre-meditated intuition

Half a dick

shallow love
just below the surface
not having to reach
not having to fall in
to exist and just exist
being still
standing in mid air
somehow still grounded

glass half empty

no words on the obvious
"i give my all"
whoa re you to judge how much you give
who I am to say what your all is
you can feel your all
I can say its enough

Shallow Minds

controlling actions with just a thought
who is he
who are his actions to you
steady pulling the gun on me
aiming for my head
consistently being who you have always been
consistently changing at the same of being the
same
your growth is those of weeds and burning fires
they say life comes after
they say weeds are bad for your your
life takes time
weeds are still flowers and beautiful
eyes of the beholder
which eyes will you chose
like a seasonal episode of "Get Out"
is it your longing to find love
your treatment of words that should have
remained unspoken
too much of gasping for air
not knowing water breathers are in your midst
imitating is a form of flattery
whats a compliment
not knowing an asumption of your unconscious
insecurity is in the bag

Typical Male Ego

needing me to build her
"i love my girlfriend"
slamming doors in her face with taxt messages
missed calls from the girl-nextdoor
Don't build her
He gone tell her he loves her
going back and forth just to show her a different
life
choosey lovers
what can you do for you
one track minded
jump the tracks
get your self back
do what you lack
He exposes your weaknesses
he love you
a rose with thorns and blossom

www.ingramcontent.com/pod-product-compliance
Lightning Source LLC
Chambersburg PA
CBHW071249140726
47996CB00007B/2821